Animal Eggs

by Molly Fleck

What You Already Know

Living things grow in different ways. Different kinds of plants and animals have different life cycles.

Most plants grow from seeds. A seed coat protects the seed. It also protects the tiny plant and the stored food that are inside the seed. A seed will germinate when it gets enough water and air. The seed will first grow into a seedling. That seedling will then grow into an adult plant.

Some animals lay eggs. Others do not. Animals such as the sea turtle and dragonfly lay eggs. Young mammals grow inside their mothers.

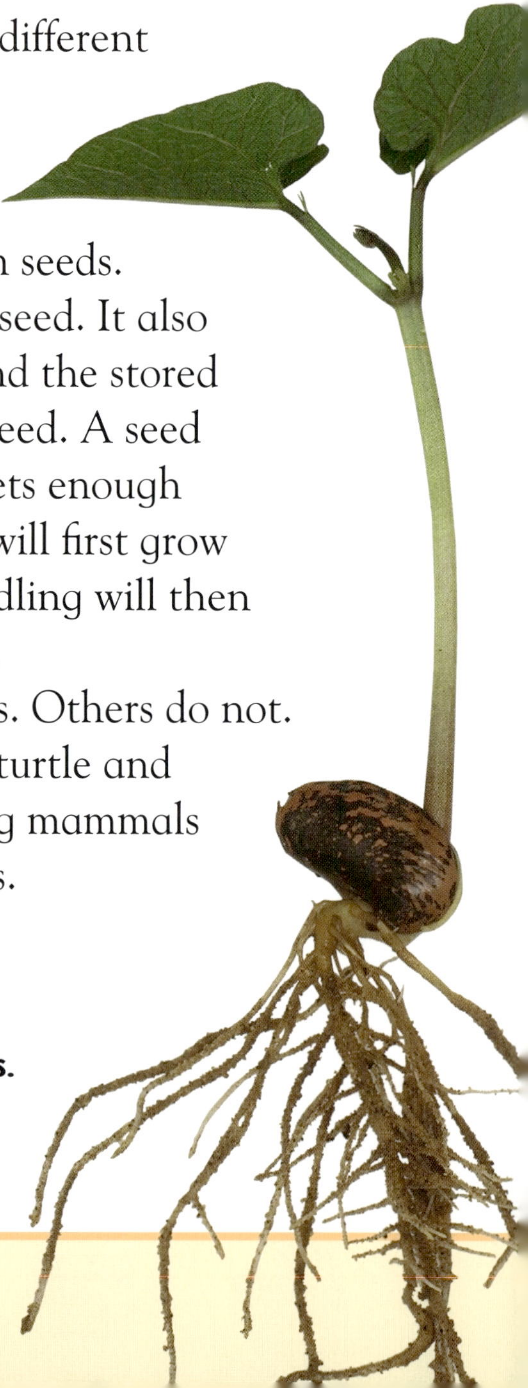

Bean plants grow from seeds.

Sea turtles live in the ocean. They crawl onto beaches to dig their nests and lay their eggs. Young sea turtles look just like their parents.

Dragonflies often lay their eggs in the water. Nymphs hatch from dragonfly eggs. They look different from their parents, and they have no wings. As nymphs grow, they shed their skin. They will grow wings by the time they reach adulthood.

This book is about many different kinds of animal eggs. You will learn about the kinds of animals that lay eggs, how some animals keep their eggs safe, and how eggs hatch.

This dragonfly has just shed its skin.

All About Eggs

Eggs keep the young animals that are growing inside them safe. They also provide food. When the young animal inside the egg is ready to hatch, it breaks out of the shell.

Birds, fish, reptiles, and amphibians lay eggs. Most insects lay eggs too. Different kinds of animals lay their eggs in different environments. Young animals can grow safely inside the eggs.

bird eggs

corn snake hatching

Eggs come in many different shapes, sizes, and colors. Some animals lay just one egg at a time. Other animals lay many eggs at once.

Bird eggs have a hard, protective shell. Many bird eggs are oval shaped. They may be a solid color or have spots on them.

Most frogs lay their eggs in water. Frogs lay a lot of eggs. Their eggs stay held in a glob of jelly. Insects such as moths and butterflies usually lay their eggs in clusters. They will sometimes lay them on leaves.

frog eggs

butterfly eggs

Growth And Development

Eggs need to be kept still and warm. Otherwise, the young animals inside them will not be able to develop and hatch. Birds incubate, or warm, their eggs by sitting on them. Most eggs get incubated in a nest. A hen incubates her eggs for twenty-one days before they hatch. The emperor penguin holds its eggs on top of its feet, under the feathers of its belly.

A hen keeps her eggs warm.

Many animals do not incubate their eggs. Instead they find a sheltered spot to lay their eggs. Eggs will often be laid beneath a rock or log.

turtle egg

Most turtles lay eggs in nests that they have dug. They throw soil on the nest to hide it. If a predator does not find the nest, the young turtles inside the eggs will develop and hatch.

Newly hatched sea turtles come out of their nest and crawl to the ocean.

Protection

Animals have many ways to keep eggs safe from predators or bad weather. Some animals use their bodies to shelter their eggs. Male seahorses carry their eggs in a pouch on the front of their bodies.

Crabs, shrimp, and lobsters are animals with many legs and a hard shell-like covering. They carry their eggs on their bellies and keep them safe until they hatch.

a velvet crab carrying its eggs

eggs in a
teal duck nest

a camouflaged
quail's egg nest

Some animals make nests to protect their eggs. Some birds use twigs, leaves, and grass to make nests. Birds such as woodpeckers drill nests with their beaks. The northern bobwhite camouflages its nest with grass.

Some eggs cannot be seen by predators because of their color or pattern. These eggs often look like rocks, stones, or other things in their habitat.

Hatching Out

While a mother or father bird is busy keeping its eggs warm, the young bird inside is growing. It feeds off the egg white and egg yolk. For the first two weeks, the young bird eats the egg white. After that, it eats the egg yolk.

A duckling has begun to hatch.

The duckling uses its beak to break through the shell.

A newly hatched duckling is wet.

Young birds use their beaks to break out of their shells and hatch. Many chicks have a special tooth called an egg tooth. This hard, sharp bump helps the chick break through the eggshell. The egg tooth falls off after the chick hatches.

This duckling is two days old.

Bird Eggs

Bird eggs come in many shapes and sizes. Ostrich eggs are round. Their shells are thick. Ostriches lay the biggest bird eggs in the world. Each egg weighs about three pounds! Hummingbirds lay the smallest eggs. A hummingbird egg is about the size of a pea.

hummingbird eggs

ostrich egg

starling

hen

cuckoo

oystercatcher

peregrine falcon

Bird eggs come in many shapes, sizes, and colors.

The color and shape of bird eggs may be adapted to their environment. Some birds lay their eggs on the ground. The eggs of these birds have spots. The spots camouflage the eggs.

Some birds, such as the guillemot (GIL-uh-mot), nest on cliffs. Their eggs are pointy at one end. This pointy shape keeps the eggs from rolling off the cliffs.

guillemot eggs

Reptile Eggs

day 1, 8:30 P.M.

day 2, 4:30 A.M.

Most reptiles are oviparous. This means they lay eggs. Some reptiles lay only one egg at a time, but others lay hundreds! Many reptiles dig nests or hide their eggs. Some reptiles remain near their eggs. Other reptiles, such as tortoises, leave their eggs to hatch.

After a tortoise has laid her eggs, they usually take about one year to hatch. The young tortoise grows up inside the egg. When the young tortoise is ready, it uses its beak to break the shell. It takes about ten hours for a tortoise to fully hatch.

A leopard tortoise hatches from its egg.

day 2, 6:20 A.M.

Alligators and crocodiles guard their nests.

Alligator and crocodile eggs are hard, like bird eggs. Snake eggs have tough, leathery shells. The eggshells stretch as the young snakes grow.

Young snakes have a special tooth on their upper jaw. Like some birds, they lose their special tooth after they hatch.

corn snake hatching

Amphibian Eggs

Most amphibians lay their eggs in water or moist ground. Amphibian eggs are held together in a glob of jelly. Most amphibians hatch as larvae. When larvae turn into adults they change a lot! This big change is called metamorphosis.

Newts hatch as larvae in water. When they change into adults they can live on land.

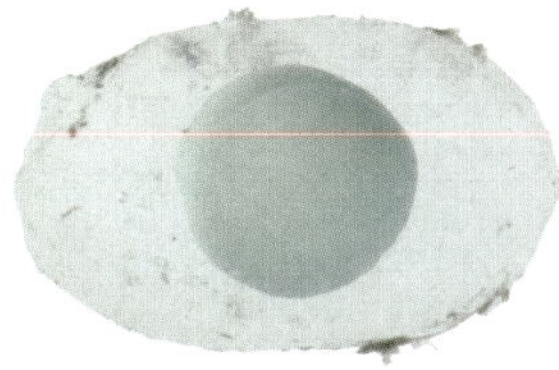

newt egg

newt hatching

an adult newt after it has gone through metamorphosis

Amphibian eggs are protected by gel-like blobs.

Most amphibians lay a lot of eggs all at once. Large bullfrogs may lay as many as forty-five thousand eggs at the same time!

A lot of amphibians do not stay with their eggs. Some frogs and toads, such as the male midwife toad, lay their eggs on land. They carry their eggs to water to hatch. One kind of Australian frog swallows its eggs. When the eggs hatch, the adult opens its mouth to let the young frogs out.

A male midwife toad carries its eggs until they hatch.

Insect Eggs

dragonfly

Insect eggs are very small. They come in many different shapes and colors. Most insect eggs are oval or round shaped. The eggs are usually white, or close to white, in color.

Some newly hatched insects look like their parents, only smaller. Others look different from their parents. These young insects are called nymphs or larvae. Their look changes as they grow into adults.

Dragonfly nymphs do not fly. Soon the nymph will become a winged, flying adult.

wasp

This wasp nest is made of thin layers of paper.

Insects lay many eggs at a time. Termites can lay up to thirty thousand eggs a day! Insects lay their eggs in many places, often on or near food. When the young hatch, their first meal is nearby.

Some wasps chew plants to make paper. They use the paper to build nests. Then they lay their eggs in the nest.

A ladybug lays its eggs on a leaf.

Fish Eggs

Some fish eggs are light. They are so light that they float on the top of the water. Other fish eggs are heavy and sink to the bottom of the water. Many fish eggs become food for hungry predators.

Some fish grow into adults in minutes. Others take years to become adults.

goldfish egg

goldfish hatching

A goldfish takes four years to become an adult.

dogfish hatching

Cod, herring, and many other fish do not stay with their eggs. However, some kinds of fish keep their eggs safe.

Trout cover their eggs with gravel before they leave them. Sticklebacks guard their eggs until they hatch. Brown bullheads will protect their young after they hatch. Some kinds of fish even carry their eggs in their mouths until they hatch.

a bullhead protecting its eggs

Many Different Eggs

Eggs come in many different sizes, colors, and shapes. Animals lay eggs in many different places. They lay eggs in water, in nests, below the ground, or on the ground. Some eggs are held in a glob of jelly. Others have a hard covering, such as a shell.

Some animals stay with their eggs until they hatch. Birds incubate their eggs so the young will grow.

snake hatching

duck hatching

Some animals guard their eggs to keep them safe. Many young animals hatch on their own.

Eggs contain the food a young animal needs to live. For many animals, an egg is the perfect place to grow.

ladybug eggs

dogfish egg case

frog eggs

Glossary

egg tooth	a special tooth that helps some young animals break out of their egg
hatch	when a young animal breaks out of its egg
incubate	keep warm to help hatch
larvae	young animals that change through metamorphosis to become adults
metamorphosis	changing from a nymph or a larva into an adult
oviparous	egg-laying